Bygone
MORPETH

INTER SYLVAS ET FLUMINA HABITANS

Morpeth market place, *c.*1820.

Bygone
MORPETH

T. H. Rowland

Phillimore

1989

Published by
PHILLIMORE & CO. LTD.,
Shopwyke Hall, Chichester, Sussex

ISBN 0 85033 727 5

Printed and bound in Great Britain by
BIDDLES LTD.
Guildford, Surrey

List of Illustrations

Acknowledgements

I wish to express my gratitude to the following for permission to reproduce illustrations: Mrs. Crossley, nos. 151-3; F. Frith & Co. Ltd., nos. 13 and 51; G. Jennings, no. 128; Northumberland County Library, no. 129; Northumberland Record Office, nos. 28 and 141; Miss I. Smail, no. 113; Society of Antiquaries, Newcastle upon Tyne, nos. 1, 8, 26, 80-82 and 92 (deposited in Northumberland Record Office); A. B. Stait, nos. 19 and 20; Mr. Telfer and the Y.M.C.A., nos. 27, 55, 57, 98, 99, 104, 106, 107, 115, 126 and 161; A. Tweddle, nos. 32, 46 and 122; Valentine & Co. (Dundee), nos. 6, 111 and 148-50; W. Wallace, nos. 38, 48-50, 59-61, 63-65, 96, 105, 110, 119, 122, 132, 135, 137, 143, 144 and 155.

I am also grateful to F. Moffatt, Mrs. Stokoe and A. Tweddle for providing information for the book; to Bob Steward for all his help; and to my wife who did the typing.

Introduction

The town of Morpeth in Northumberland is situated on a loop of the river Wansbeck, about a dozen miles from the sea at Cambois. The river has always played an important part in the town's history, periodically overflowing its banks. Little is known about Morpeth, except archaeologically, until the Norman Conquest. There was a prehistoric hill fort on the high ground to the east and a number of Romano-British farmsteads scattered around. The Romans may have built a road in the area but no evidence has been found.

The name Morpeth, according to place name experts, means 'murder path', from the French *mort* meaning death. 'Newcastle' was named by the Norman conquerors, and Morpeth, too, had acquired a castle by 1095. William Rufus 'Then strengthened the Newcastle, next took Morpathe, a strong castle, which was situated on a little mound'.

The castle was a motte and timber type, which overlooked the river crossing. It would seem that the Anglo-Saxon settlement was to the west along the ridge called 'Kirkhill'. The word is an example of tautology as kirk is derived from 'cruc' meaning hill. Churches were often built on high places, previously used by pagans for their worship. It is likely that a Saxon church preceded the Norman church and the town lay between church and castle. However, the Norman barons, the de Merlays, encouraged settlement on the north side of the river. Morpeth has been described by Beresford as a perfect example of a planned medieval town. There is the distinct street plan, with the burgages or tenements stretching at right angles to the streets. The houses were on the street front and the long strips behind could be used for cultivation. The streets were, as now, Bridge Street, Oldgate and Newgate, 'gate' meaning a way or road and not a portal or barrier. The burgesses shared in the use of the common fields and tradesmen were always part-time farmers.

An important development occurred in 1138. Ranulph de Merlay had stayed at Fountains Abbey and was so impressed by the piety of the Cistercian monks that he brought a group of them to Morpeth and they stayed at his castle. This resulted in the building of the Abbey of Newminster, taking its name from the 'new town' of Morpeth with its 'Newgate'. Important people were buried at Newminster and many members of the royal family stayed there until it was demolished in the time of Henry VIII. Since it was not converted into a country house as were many religious institutions, it was plundered by the townspeople; much abbey stone was used to build Morpeth houses. Eventually only a solitary arch and broken walls remained.

Trade developed in Morpeth, and in 1199 King John granted a Charter giving Borough status. The burgesses had control of the market and other affairs, but were still subjects of the lord of the manor. In 1202 John had visited the town, but after the signing of Magna Carta in 1215, reacted angrily against the northern barons, including Roger de Merlay. Morpeth Castle and town were destroyed by fire. By this time a stone-built castle existed on another site.

The parish church of St Mary was rebuilt in this period, but it was situated a considerable distance from the main part of the town, now north of the river. There may have been a wooden bridge, but by the time of Edward I something more substantial was needed.

The King was engaged in Scottish affairs and needed better communications. This may have prompted the burgesses to build a two-arched stone bridge, the central pier of which still stands. Connected with this was the Chantry Chapel of All Saints at the north end of the bridge, where prayers could be said for native and stranger, for the living and the dead. Tolls were taken for the maintenance of the bridge.

By this time the de Greystock family had acquired Morpeth lands by marriage, and the Scottish Wars were being waged from 1298. There was increased trade, and increasing danger, so the castle was rebuilt and strengthened. Tax levies in 1296 shows that Morpeth had 35 taxpayers, including 12 jurors. Others were foresters, a fuller, a weaver, cobblers, a salter, fishermen, clerics, a glover and a smith. These constituted only a small part of the population.

A document of 1523 shows how the town crafts had developed and guilds were formed. There were seven guilds, for merchants and taylors; tanners; fullers, dyers, carvers and hatters; smiths, saddlers and armourers; cordwainers; weavers; and skinners, glovers and butchers. The free burgesses were freemen and chosen in a fixed proportion from the guilds, subject to the approval of the lord of the manor. They voted in local elections and, from 1553 when Edward VI granted a charter for town and school, they could vote in Parliamentary elections for two members of Parliament. By the Reform Act of 1832 the borough was reduced to one member, and in 1835 the Borough Council was reformed.

Thomas, Lord Dacre, had acquired Morpeth by marriage to Elizabeth, the Greystock heiress. In 1503 he received Princess Margaret at Morpeth on her way north to marry James IV of Scotland. Ten years later he fought at Flodden where James IV was killed, and in 1515 he received Queen Margaret at Harbottle Castle. There she gave birth to a daughter and was taken for a time to stay in Morpeth Castle.

Lord Thomas, who died in 1525, and his son, Lord William Dacre, were both in turn Wardens of the Marches, having to deal with the Scots and border thieves from Tynedale and Redesdale. At times the castle was used as a prison and there was also a stronghouse in Bridge Street, which became the Old Gaol.

In 1569 George, the young Lord Dacre, was killed by the fall of a wooden horse, and his three sisters had been married to three sons of the Duke of Norfolk. Lord William Howard married Elizabeth Dacre, becoming Lord of Morpeth and Gilsland. In 1604 he presented to Morpeth Borough the mace, which is still one of its treasures.

'Belted Will' died in 1640 and so did not see his country torn by Civil War. Morpeth was invaded several times, and in 1644 Scottish supporters of Parliament occupied Morpeth Castle. They were besieged by Royalist Scots under Montrose, and cleared the outer bailey of buildings except the great barn. Montrose battered the castle walls with great and small cannon and effected a breach. In the process, the walls and gatehouse were severely damaged and buildings in the inner courtyard were razed, leaving it in a ruinous condition. The Howard heir became a colonel in Cromwell's army and met an American, George Downing, its 'master spy'. They collaborated later in brixnging about the restoration of Charles II. Colonel Howard, already Lord Howard, became the Earl of Carlisle, recovering his lands. Downing, M.P. for Morpeth, was knighted and served the King in foreign affairs and by reforming the Treasury. He was rewarded with land and wealth – Downing Street was his property.

The Howards did not reside in Morpeth, so that it has no 17th- or 18th-century mansion. However, the Earl of Carlisle (1706) did provide the town with a grand town hall, and his architect was Vanbrugh. Vanbrugh designed Seaton Delaval for the Delavals and Castle Howard in Yorkshire for the Earl of Carlisle. Carlisle accounts show that produce and animals were regularly sent from Morpeth to Naworth as well as financial payments. Articles were shipped from London to Newcastle and then transferred via Morpeth to Cumbria. The greatest financial return came from the letting of the Morpeth mills, and townspeople were compelled to use them. There was also coal mining near Morpeth, and in 1736 a survey was made of the Wansbeck from Cambois to Morpeth, noting mills, weirs and other obstructions, with a view to cutting a canal and making Morpeth a port. But it did not prove possible and, in a time of bad roads, the waggonway was a more satisfactory form of transport. In the 18th century roads were much improved by Turnpike Trusts, using the methods of Telford and Macadam. Morpeth became an important staging post on the Great North Road for mail and the conveyance of people. Horses were changed while the driver and passengers enjoyed a quick drink. Hostelries like the *Queen's Head* and the *Black Bull* were important. The *Black Bull* had stabling for 80 horses. John Scott, later Lord Eldon, and his wife Bessie Surtees stayed at the *Queen's Head* on returning from their elopement to Scotland.

With increasing traffic by road, Morpeth (as in modern times) became a bottleneck and coaches were overturned on the narrow hump-backed bridge. Consequently, a very fine bridge, engineered by Thomas Telford and designed by John Dobson, was built by Mr. King in 1831. It has carried traffic ever since and the Chantry Bridge was demolished.

John Dobson was also responsible at this time for designing the new County Gaol in castle-style after a study of the architecture of Welsh castles. There was a great gatehouse, with walls 20 ft. high and apartments for all manner of offenders within. Some visitors approved and others, like Cobbett, were appalled at the waste of public money.

Morpeth had developed into one of the greatest cattle markets in the country, not only for local cattle but also for drove cattle from Scotland. On market days cattle thronged the streets, and other animals were penned on the pavements. Countrymen came in their carts and waggons, which were left in the streets, while the horses were stabled at the many inns, taverns, hotels and beerhouses – some fifty in number. To quote one visitor, Edmund Bogg,

> On market days and fairs, Morpeth is aroused from its slumbers and it is very curious to watch the humble jumble of humanity. At such times herds of shaggy cattle and droves of sheep are huddled in the streets, horses are trotted hither and thither to show off their paces: dogs are heard barking and yelping furiously: old cattle drovers – unique specimens of humanity – shuffle before our eyes like the sole survivors of a bygone generation, each carrying a stout stick, whooping, gesticulating and yelling at the pent up cattle, forming a veritable pandemonium. Cumbrous wagons, drawn by powerful horses, lumber slowly through the streets, vehicles of various descriptions containing farmers, their wives and daughters roll up to the various inns for the occupants to alight: and thus they come and the town grows into a ceaseless uproar of traffic and bargaining.

The market was somewhat reduced by the advent of railways from 1850 onwards, but horse-drawn vehicles were still very much in use, and animals still travelled on their own feet. Many animals were slaughtered in Morpeth to provide for local butchers and tanners. There were a number of tanneries in the town, and oak bark was an important ingredient for preserving skins as leather. At one time Bothal Castle was used as an oak bark store for Morpeth tanners and the woods around were systematically copsed. Trees and woods were used, so that the Morpeth motto *Inter Sylvas et Flumina Habitans* (Living amid the Woods and Waters) was not just a tourist advertisement. William Howitt wrote of Morpeth as 'always more like a town in a dream than actuality'.

The 'miasma' revealed by the Sanitary Report of 1849 was something very different, showing the shocking conditions in which many people lived. The Public Health Act of 1848, introduced into Parliament by Lord Morpeth, had made it obligatory to conduct an enquiry if the death rate rose above a certain level. There was an outbreak of cholera in Lumsden's Lane where people lived above privies, ashpits and pigsties. There was no drainage, refuse was piled up and stinking pools lay about. Things were not improved by some of the smells and waste emanating from the butchers' shops and tanneries.

It was vital to make a sanitary survey, improve the drainage system and also the water supply. Much local water came from springs and wells, but Thomas King had constructed waterworks to the south of the town. In 1832 gasworks were established and in 1849 there were 25 public lights from sunset to sunrise, except during full moon and 14 summer weeks. Things were improving.

Some changes in the townscape were taking place. The Rev. Francis Grey was determined to have a new church built, and from 1846 the Church of St James the Great was built in Norman style. The Chantry was considered unsafe for services and St Mary's was too far from the main part of the town.

William Woodman, the town clerk, had, after a prolonged legal battle, won an award of £15,000 for the Grammar School. It was decided to build a new school on Cottingwood Lane: Benjamin Ferry was the architect for this, as for the church. The Chantry was sold and after a time was put to industrial uses – in 1872 it became the Mineral Water Manufactory.

In 1854 the Mackay family brought out the weekly *Morpeth Herald* with national and local news. The Crimean War figured in the first issue. The paper continued in the hands of the same family until a few years ago, when Tweeddale Press took over.

The gatehouse of the castle was restored and the town hall was rebuilt in 1869-70, still keeping the Vanbrugh style. Perhaps the most prominent new building in the town was the County Pauper Lunatic Asylum.

It occupies an elevated site about half a mile from the town and is visible for miles around. It is a large and handsome building in the Italian style, of red brick, with stone dressing, erected in 1853-9, at a cost of £54,350 inclusive of the 99 acres on which it is built. This land is laid out in pleasure grounds, kitchen gardens and farm land, the cultivation of which affords employment to many of the inmates, whilst others work at the trades in which they have been previously employed. There is accommodation for 450 patients. In 1864 a handsome chapel was erected for the use of the inmates, at a cost of £1,150, in which service is held daily by the chaplain. The treatment of each patient is based on his or her mental idiosyncracies. Systematic occupation, exercise and amusement form a leading feature in the system and already many a deranged mind has been restored to its normal condition.

Between 1865 and 1866 a new workhouse was built in a prominent position on Newgate Street. The coming of the railway brought more shops to Bridge Street and a decline in Newgate Street, where some of the houses became decrepit and overcrowded lodging houses.

A number of new churches were built, including a Catholic church in 1850 in Oldgate, next to Collingwood's House, and dedicated to St Robert, first abbot of Newminster. The Presbyterians had met in Horsley's chapel (Cottingwood) since 1721, but from 1861 they had a new church – St George's on the site of the Manorial Mill. It is interesting to notice that these two churches had spires, whereas both Anglican churches had towers. Both the Primitive Methodists and Wesleyan Methodists had chapels in Manchester Street.

Some of the old crafts were declining, but from 1864 more employment was provided by the establishment of Swinney's Ironworks on the site of a tanyard on the Cotting Burn. Here all kinds of castings and ironwork were made, and the works continued for more than a century. The Swinneys helped to establish a new Congregational chapel in Dacre Street. This and Howard Road were new housing developments to the north-east of the town.

Many trees were planted in 1887 for Queen Victoria's Jubilee and great celebrations took place. One of the features of Morpeth was the extent of private gardens and market gardens with many orchard trees. Matheson's gardens in Oldgate were famous, extending all along the river. The Mechanics' Institute was given accommodation in the town hall and, in memory of the 7th Earl of Carlisle, it was presented with a telescope, microscope and 75 books, one of which was Turner's *Herbal*, now one of the town's proudest possessions. A later Earl of Carlisle handed over the administration of his estates to his wife, the Countess Rosalind. She was a feminist and reformer, determined to show that she could take over a man's job. She had only female staff in her house – the males were employed outdoors. She was in favour of temperance and considered that male employees drank too much. Since the Morpeth estates did not pay, she decided to sell and in 1887 large areas of property were put on the market, but not all were sold. The town hall did not fetch the asking price and when later it was offered to the Borough Council, the unacceptable condition was 'no drinking on the premises'. Lord Joicey came to the rescue, purchased the building and presented it to the town (1915). In fairness to the Countess Rosalind, it should be said that she presented the town with the area now called Carlisle Park and some woodland.

Bulmer's *Directory* of 1888 provides interesting information about Morpeth Town. The old crafts had declined in importance, but there was still a variety of tradespeople, serving the town and the adjoining countryside. There were 14 butchers, four bakers, six blacksmiths, 15 boot and shoe makers, with two clogmakers, two coopers and 10 confectioners; 11 cart-owners supplemented the work of 23 carriers. Horses were still very much in use despite the railways, and the automobile was yet to come. There were three corn millers and 17 cowkeepers with 13 farmers. Grocers numbered 22, haberdashers seven, hatters four and hairdressers the same. There were 28 inns, hotels and beerhouses with three wine and spirit merchants and two brewers. Mr. Jobling of the *George and Dragon* had built his battlemented Howard Castle in Dacre Street, and another fine building was Winton House, where Mr. Davison lived later. A number of prominent people with business elsewhere had houses in Morpeth. Mr. William Jobling, shipowner and engineer, lived at Norse Villa, and he must have known Walter Runciman, another shipowner. Runciman's monument of a Viking adorns the entrance to the present day County Hall. The 'hardy Norseman' image appealed to both men.

The Honourable and Reverend Francis Grey lived at the Old Rectory near St Mary's church. He was the son of Earl Grey of the Reform Bill, and had many visiting friends and relations, so that the rectory had to be very much extended. His wife was a daughter of the Earl of Carlisle. The Rev. Ellis of Bothal was related both to the Howards and the Duke of Portland. The Rector of Bothal had a town house in Morpeth, as did Charles Fenwick, M.P. for Newcastle.

For a very long period the Howards had dominated the political life of the town, and until 1832 one of the Howards was an M.P. and the other member was often a relative. There were always aristocratic connections and sons of peers first made their way into the House of Commons at considerable cost. From 1796 to 1802 William Huskisson was M.P. for Morpeth with the Hon. George Howard. Huskisson was later killed on 15 September 1830 at the ceremonial opening of the Liverpool to Manchester Railway. After 1832 the political scene was more peaceful with William Ord, followed by Sir George Grey. Then came a great shock. In 1868 the vote was extended, so that many working men, including miners, were enfranchised. Morpeth, surrounded by mines including the Howard pits at Netherton, was combined with Bedlington as a constituency. Thomas Burt, the Northumberland and Miners' Secretary, was adopted at Bedlington, and in 1874 in a rousing contest he defeated the Conservative, Major Duncan.

Burt, with Alexander Macdonald, the Scottish miners' leader, became the first working class M.P. He rose from pitman to Parliament and was a Privy Councillor. He served Morpeth for more than forty years, and often addressed miners' picnics in the town. Earl Grey descriccbed him as 'the finest gentleman I ever knew'. He was a teetotaller and a devout Methodist, very considerate to his fellow men and is still remembered with affection.

There were further extensions of housing with terraces of houses on the North Fields, suitable for all classes. Other expanding residential areas were West Greens and Tenter Terrace – a reminder of weaving and the cloth trade. In Manchester Street, where there was once a manufactory, a Primitive Methodist chapel was built in 1871 and a Wesleyan Methodist chapel in 1884. Quite near were the St James's Schools (Anglican) and the Borough Schools with some rivalry between them. St George's Presbyterian church had taken the site of the Manorial Mill, and for some years the Wauk Mill was converted into a hostelry called the *Prince Albert*. It was run by Tommy and then John Longstaffe, who had a museum and a menagerie. The inn did not long survive Prince Albert himself, but the field is still called Tommy's Field, and reminds us that each of the inns provided pasturage for their clients' animals as well as ordinary hospitality. Street space was also rented for market days, and it was difficult to get about at such times.

Railway traffic had increased considerably and an ornamental glazed tile map at Morpeth Station shows their full extent in 1904. There was the Blyth and Tyne line to the coast, and in the summer many Morpethians went to stay at Newbiggin or travelled west on day trips. From 1862 the Wanney Line continued to Redesmouth, where it linked with the Hexham line. Travellers could go southwards, or northwards to Scotland. Another line linked Morpeth via Scots Gap to Rothbury. This was specially valuable later when the Fontburn Reservoir was built. Besides the passenger trains, all kinds of goods were carried, including coal, stone and cattle. Military men and materials could be conveyed to West Woodburcn for the Otterburn Range. Many main line expresses passed through Morpeth on the Newcastle to Edinburgh line. These were the great days of steam, as yet unthreatened by the automobile. Soon, however, Colonel Mitford appeared with a magnificent machine, and Septimus Jennings proceeded like William Morris of Oxford from cycles to motor cars. But his models were Fords, and Jennings still fly the same standard.

From 1881 the County Gaol moved to Newcastle, and the Morpeth buildings and grounds were sold. However, the Court House was retained and other buildings were used as Police Headquarters. Some of the stone of the outer walls was used for building elsewhere, and Goosehill Council Schools were constructed partly on gaol property.

In 1890 the Rev. Francis Grey died. He and his wife Elizabeth had done an immense amount of good work for the town and its people. He could have moved to better preferments, but stayed on. St James's church was his proudest work. After his death a monumental arcade was built on Newgate Street, leading through the avenue of lime trees to the west end of the church. It is rather delicately constructed with columns of Frosterley marble. The iron gates are inscribed: 'To the Glory of God in the memory of the Hon. and Rev. Francis Richard Grey, son of Charles, second Earl Grey of Howick, who died March 22nd. 1890. Aged 77 years. This gateway is erected by parishioners and friends.' Above the arches on the stonework is incised 'Lord I have loved the Habitation of Thy House and the place where Thine Honour dwelleth'. A century later we are faced with the question – 'What will be the fate of this House of God?' A town, three times as large as that of 1888, finds it difficult to sustain three Anglican churches. Morpeth's population in 1888 was given as 5,068; it is now about 15,000.

It is necessary, very briefly, to sketch a century of change. In 1888 County Councils were established by law and it is hard to visualise the multiplicity of boards, committees and organisations that carried out their present functions. There were many voluntary societies providing for public needs including education. There were Church Schools, Board Schools, Borough Schools and private 'academies'. The County Council tended to assume control after 1902, and in 1911 the Goosehill Council Schools opened on the gaol site for 200 girls and 245 boys.

The town had celebrated Queen Victoria's Jubilees of 1887 and 1897. But sadness came from the casualties of the Boer War, in which a number of Morpethians served. 'Mafeking Night' was celebrated with bonfires as a great victory and a small park was given that name. In 1900 a double row of terraced houses from Oldgate behind the Market to the river was named Pretoria Avenue. One soldier who served under Colonel Vaux was W. S. Sanderson, who later prospered in brewing and property. He was proprietor of the *Queen's Head* and was a councillor, alderman and four times mayor. His portrait hangs in the town hall, and he is remembered as 'Mr. Morpeth'.

The Mechanics' Institute had started in the *Scotch Arms Inn*, which filled the gap that now exists between the town hall and the Midland Bank. The premises were used by the British Workman, a social club, and the Young Men's Christian Association, which started as early as 1876. Such associations were important in the development of the town and what might be called 'further education'. The Y.M.C.A. attracted much support, and the President, Alderman G. B. Bainbridge, purchased the property called Watson's Corner. On this was erected the most outstanding building of the town, rising above the clock tower and rivalling the town hall. On 2 February 1905 the premises were formally opened by Lord Armstrong. The large recreation room was called Bainbridge Hall, and was suitable for all kinds of functions including religious services. Among the many activities was the Annual Exhibition. In 1911 this was opened by Viscountess Ridley of Blagdon. The President said that the purpose of the Association was 'the development of all round manhood, by recognising the needs of the body, mind and spirit'. (Meanwhile the Suffragettes, including local Emily Davison, were agitating for the rights of women.) The work of the Association was mentioned – the territorial camps, the work of the boys and other activities. A special hymnal had been produced for the Y.M.C.A. The entertainment on this occasion was a recital of poems, including Macaulay's 'Horatius', and a lantern lecture with 100 glass slides. There was a flourishing photographic society and the exhibition consisted of photographs and slides, submitted in various sections – some open and some confined to members. There were 200 exhibits, and at this time the Association had 250 members. Bible classes were held as well as Sunday services. There was a Reading Room with books, magazines and newspapers. Groups included a male voice choir and a hockey club, a literary and debating society and a St John's Ambulance first aid class. There were excursions and annual conventions on a world-wide basis. By 1907 Vice Presidents had included 13 J.P.s and 3 M.P.s – T. Burt, C. Fenwick and C. P. Trevelyan.

The Y.M.C.A. was involved deeply in the 1914-18 war supplying men and providing for troops. Eighteen members were killed, and in 1921 Alderman G. B. Bainbridge unveiled a memorial tablet to them. The town war memorial was erected on Castle Bank looking towards the station. It was said to be the last view men would see on leaving and the first to be seen on return. In the First World War 232 local men did not return and in the Second 77 died. Remembrance services are held annually on 11 November.

In November 1955 the Y.M.C.A. held its Golden Jubilee celebrations in their headquarters at Morpeth. Esther McCracken, the dramatist whose father Harry Armstrong was one of the founders, opened the fair and exhibition. The President, Mr. Cuthbert Bainbridge, aged 80, the same age as the Association, said that it had been justified by its work in two wars and the years between. The camera club had provided a photographic exhibition of Old Morpeth, work which had progressed over a number of years. Some 50 years of the town's history was shown in black and white – colour photography was not yet popular. There were pictures of cattle in the streets, the horse traffic, the old shops and people in the fashions of the time. Included were celebrations and pastimes, weddings and funerals. Buildings, whether stone or brick, were blackened by years of smoke from coal fires and their many chimneys.

Since then things have changed. Morpeth is a smokeless area, and many houses have been cleaned by sand-blasting and the natural processes of wind and weather. Gaslight in houses and streets has been replaced by electricity. In 1955 the gaslighter still went round on his bicycle with a long pole. The horses that pulled coal carts and milk floats have gone, and so have the many steam trains.

The cattle mart came to an end a year or two ago and houses are being built on the site. Morpeth is no longer a cattle town. Motor cars became the curse of the streets and the by-pass has only given partial relief. Housing estates have been developed in each extended quarter of the town. The central part has been cleared for car parks and shopping areas. The building extensions on all the burgages have been bulldozed and shopping premises are not usually inhabited. The old back-yards and courts have mostly gone, but some of the old passages like 'Horse Entry' can still be seen. The tanyards have gone, Swinney's Ironworks have closed and the mills work no more. There is a large industrial estate in the area of the station and Searles Pharmaceutical Factory rises to the west. The common is still grazed by cattle, but part of it has become the golf course. There are still extensive woodlands along the Wansbeck Valley westwards to Mitford and eastwards to Bothal, providing pleasant walks.

In 1974 came a great change in local government. Morpeth Borough was combined with Castle Ward to become Castle Morpeth Borough Council, a much extended area including Ponteland. The county administrative offices have moved to Morpeth on the southern outskirts of the town. The buildings were officially opened by the Prince of Wales in 1982. G. N. Wright in *View of Northumbria* (1981) states, 'With the new County of Northumberland, excluding Newcastle, Morpeth has assumed the mantle of county town and administrative centre, with various county services having headquarters there'.

It is still a fair town, and P. Anderson Graham's book *Highways and Byways in Northumbria*, reprinted in 1988, speaks of 'the ancient and attractive town of Morpeth, thought by some to be the most beautiful town of Northumberland'.

Sources of Information

Borough Records deposited in the County Record Office.

The Woodman Collection belonging to the Newcastle Society of Antiquaries in the County Record Office.

Hodgson's *History of Morpeth*: introduction by H. Rowland, republished by Frank Graham.

Mate's *Guide to Morpeth*, 1908. Text by James Ferguson.

Morpeth Trails Nos. 1-8 by A. Tweddle.

Visit Historic Morpeth by H. Rowland.

History of the Morpeth Gas Company, 1933.

Howard Records, deposited at Durham Department of Palaeography.

Morpet a market towne is XII long miles from NewCastle. Wansbeke a praty ryver rynnithe thrughe the syde of the towne. On the hethar syde of the river is the principall churche of the towne. On the same syde is the fayre castle stonding upon a hill, longinge with the towne to the Lord Dacres of Gilsland. The towne is longe and metely well buyldyd with low houses, the stretes pavyd. It is a far fayrar towne than Alenwike.

Leland, c.1540

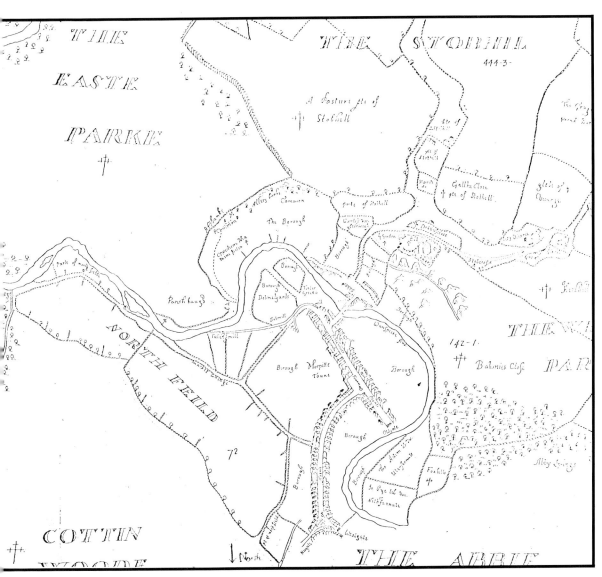

1. Map made in 1604 by John Haiwarde for Lord William Howard of Naworth. The demesne lands are marked with crosses. The map is orientated with south at the top. The streets are plainly shown and the castle has a large tower within the walls.

2. Newminster Abbey, abode of Cistercian monks, founded in 1138, was destroyed 400 years later by Henry VIII. Only ruins remained, but 'the fragments which remain prove that in beauty and refinement of detail it was the equal of any building in the North' (H. Honeyman, architect and antiquarian, 1949).

3. Newminster Abbey: this engraving of a painting by Luke Clennell, *c.* 1800, shows only the north doorway standing as a romantic ruin. Stones had gone to build Morpeth and the remains were underground. Some excavations were made in 1878 by Rev. Fowler and the masonry revealed was fenced by iron rails.

Newminster Abbey

Morpeth.

4. The ruined arch of Newminster is shown on a postcard (postmarked 1909), which is taken from a framed picture. Iron railings exclude the cattle from some parts.

. Excavations were carried out at Newminster in 1913 by Sir George Renwick, who lived at Springhill overlooking the ite. The area was developed into monastery gardens with roses and flowerbeds. This view shows rebuilding in process.

NEWMINSTER ABBEY RUINS, MORPETH.

G.9919 N

Gateway Morpeth Castle.

Arms on Sergeants Mace.

6. This photograph shows that the rebuilding of the arcade round the cloister had been completed. The top of the walls is shown as sharp and disused stone is lying aside. A lot of the glazed tiles of the floors have been lost and stone coffins were used for other purposes.

7. Morpeth Castle in a ruinous state from J. Hodgson's *History of Morpeth*. The coats of arms shown from the mace, given to the town by Lord William Howard (1604), are 1. England, King James I; 2. Howard; 3. Thomas, Duke of Norfolk; 4. de Mowbray; 5. de Mowbray; 6. de Merley; 7. Dacre; 8. Greystock; 9. Grimthorpe; 10. Howard. These families were related to the Howards who acquired their properties.

Morpeth Castle, 1777, by Thomas Hearne (1744-1806), who worked with William Byrne on *The Antiquities of Britain*. Of 52 of his engravings, eight were of Northumberland and Durham. He was considered an excellent exponent of the 'picturesque'. The original was a watercolour and shows the castle as a romantic ruin.

9. Naworth Castle, from Scott's *Border Antiquities*. A strong border hold was constructed by Lord William Howard, 'Belte
Will', much admired by Scott as a scholar and bringer of peace to the border in the time of James I. The Earl of Carlisl
still lives at Naworth Castle. Howards were buried at nearby Lanercost Abbey.

10. Ha' Hill was Morpeth's first castle, a motte and bailey structure built in Norman times. It was
described as a strong castle in 1095, but was built of timber and later destroyed. In the 12th century
the castle transferred to its present site, ravaged by King John in 1215 and during the Civil War in 1644.
The buildings within the walls were destroyed.

11. The Postern Burn, a deep ravine, separates Ha' Hill and the later castle, which was restored by the Earl of Carlisle as a residence *c*. 1850. The thorn bushes on the slope seem menacing. From the top of the gatehouse are splendid views of the town. The area in front of the gatehouse was the outer bailey.

12. This photograph shows the gatehouse on the left and the crumbling walls of the enclosure. At least four different periods of stonework can be detected. The walls are being repaired by the Landmark Trust and so this evidence has disappeared. There is a deep moat at the west end of the enclosure and old trees are being removed.

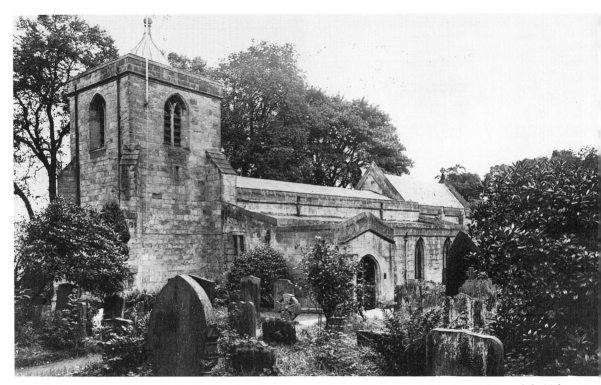

13. St Mary's church. Dowsing has indicated earlier structures beneath the present church, which is mainly 14th-centur in appearance. It is situated almost a mile from the centre of the town. There is medieval ironwork on the doors and beautiful medieval glass in the Jesse window at the east end. It has an impressive tower.

14. Inside the nave, old pews and galleries have been removed, making it more spacious. To the left of the chancel arch is a hagioscope or squint. The chancel contains sedilia with decorated canopies and the aumbry door has medieval ironwork. The main beauty of the church is the light through the eastern Jesse window, restored in memory of the Rev. John Bolland, once curate.

15.   The aisled nave and the tall chancel of St Mary's church. Some of the window-heads are monolithic, that is, carved out of one piece of stone. The graveyard contains a variety of monuments.

16.   The watch house was erected in 1831 to protect the cemetery against grave robbers. Morpeth was conveniently situated on the Edinburgh coach road, and fresh corpses fetched a good price among the medical men. A slightly tipsy drover mutttering 'She was a fine body ...' was arrested, but it turned out that he was looking for a lost cow!

17. On a rather dirty main road a carter is waiting for his picture to be taken. This shows the 'dished' wheels of his cart. Above him is the lychgate, erected in 1861 as a memorial to A. R. Fenwick, a church benefactor. The Jesse window of the church is plainly visible.

8. The old chantry bridge, which dates from the 13th century, from Hodgson's *History of Morpeth*. The weir retained water for the manorial mill which stood to the right beyond the chantry building which can be seen. The bridge, a coach hazard, was demolished after the Telford Bridge was built (1831).

9. In 1972 the pier of the medieval bridge was being undermined by water, and while repairs were made the author was allowed to excavate. The stone pier had been built on a wooden cradle of half-lapped oak timbers. The longest existing piece was 30 ft. long and 15 in. thick with bark still on it.

20. The oak timbers were held in position by piles, a metre long, and the heavy overlapping timbers can be seen. A mark on the stonework shows the amount of material that had to be removed. A concrete wall was set about the pier and the timbers were trimmed, then covered up by stonework.

21. The Chantry Chapel of All Saints. This was a remarkably long medieval church, which originally had transepts and lancet windows. It ceased to be a church when St James's was built, and was converted into a shopping complex and a mineral water manufactory. St George's Presbyterian church (1861) can be seen on the left of the picture.

22. Chantry building, north side. This part was called Collingwood House, often confused with Collingwood's House in Oldgate. The butcher and refreshment man are posing, together with the dog. Young's mineral manufactory is in the other part of the building. King Edward VI Grammar School occupied this site until 1859.

23. (*above left*) The main entrance to the Chantry building was at the west end under the bell cote. The old bell inscribed *Ave Maria Plena Gratia* (Hail Mary, full of Grace), was transferred to the new school on Cottingwood, where it can still be seen. The Chantry, described in Pevsner (1987) as a Ladies Lavatory and Mineral Manufactory, now houses the Bagpipe Museum, Crafts Centre and Tourist Information Office.

24. (*above right*) The footbridge built on the medieval pier to replace the old bridge. It was constructed in 1864 by Swinney's of Morpeth and paid for by public subscription. The bridge leads past the west end of the Chantry to Bridge Street.

25. The Chantry was extended in the 18th century by an additional building in Gothic style. This, with galleries, provided extra seating for worshippers. John Dobson also made alterations in the 19th century. The view is taken from the Telford Bridge, built in 1831.

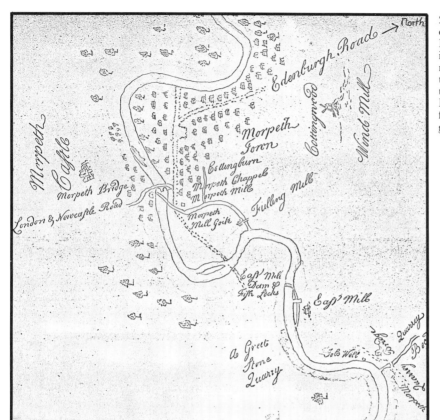

26. This map was part of a survey of the River Wansbeck made by Richard Ellison and Ralph Fowler in 1738 with a view to inland navigation. Morpeth would be the terminus – coal and stone could be transported by water. It shows East Mill where there would be the fifth lock, but navigation would not go so far as the Chantry weir.

27. East Mill was shown on the 1604 map and was rebuilt in 1798. The other large building to the right of the photograph was erected in 1892. It was unusual in having water power, then steam power which provided electricity for the mill and a number of street lights. Since milling ceased, it has been used for a variety of purposes.

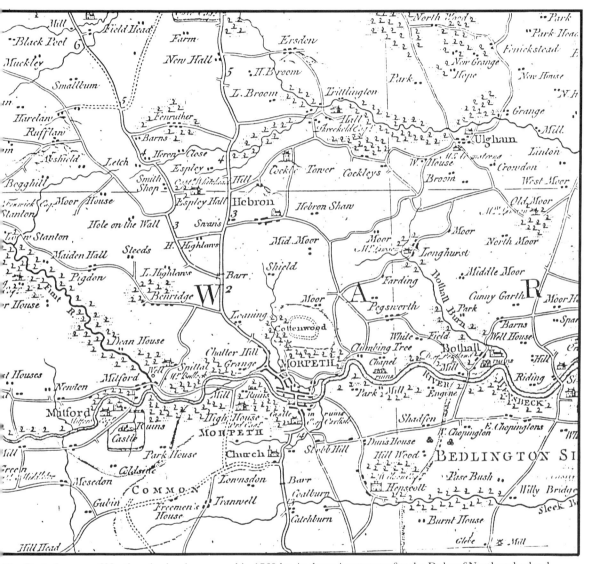

28. Part of a map of Northumberland, surveyed in 1769 by Andrew Armstrong for the Duke of Northumberland. Mitford, Morpeth and Bothal Castles are 'in ruins'. Mills and toll bars are shown, with a windmill at Cottingwood near Morpeth race course. Newminster belonged to Mr. Orde of Whitfield, who had a Morpeth residence at High House.

29. The windmill at Cottingwood, a well
known landmark in an interesting
environmental area. It was needlessly
demolished when the new school was
built. There might have been a windmill
here in Turner's time. Morpeth has had
many water mills through the ages.

30. Morpeth was a posting station on
the Great North Road from London to
Edinburgh, and coaches called here. On
18 November 1772 John Scott eloped
from Newcastle with Bessie Surtees, a
banker's daughter. They stayed at the
Queen's Head, Morpeth on their return.
John Scott was later Lord Chancellor
Eldon and knew Cuthbert Collingwood
who lived at Morpeth.

31. The *Queen's Head Hotel* is shown here after being given a face-lift in the 1930s by Alderman Sanderson. The mock-Tudor style with black timbers and white infill was very popular. Appleby's shop and the *Grey Nag's Head* had received similar treatment.

32. In the later 18th century roads were much improved by Telford and Macadam. Turnpike Trusts which made the improvements obtained a return from their investment by taking tolls at the bar. A century later, by the time of County Councils (1889), this had ceased, but the toll house remained.

North Gate
Toll Bar
North Road

33. The *Grey Nag's Head* was considered by Tomlinson (1888) as having been built to an E-plan in Tudor times, but during demolition the earliest part of the building was dated to the 17th century with the wings added later. Morpeth's inns were of vital importance to farmers and householders coming to the market, and horses were stabled here.

34. This narrow passage from Newgate Street is called Horse Entry. Farmers and those attending the market would unharness their horses and leave wheeled vehicles in the street. The horses would be taken to inn stables. Schoolboys coming in from the country would stable their ponies for the day.

The *Old Red Bull* is another well known
[in]n, situated on the Cottingburn, which joins
[th]e mill leat near here. There was a steam
[mi]ll to the left and further down the burn
[ne]ar the Wansbeck was the Wauk or Fulling
[M]ill, which was converted into the *Prince
[Alb]ert Inn*. The proprietor was Tommy
[Lo]ngstaffe.

The *Black Bull* has a notice inside
[in]dicating that it had stabling for 80 horses
[in] 1780. It was used by coaches and carriers.
[It]s name is a reminder that Morpeth was the
[gr]eatest market for black cattle in the north.
[Th]e hotel had an attractive Regency front
[ad]ded to it.

37. The *Black and Grey* is another reminder of the market and horse traffic. Newgate Street had some fine 18th-century houses, and the upper part was called Silver Street. Copper Chare off to the right is a narrow street, leading eastwards.

38. The toll house was erected to take tolls from the new bridge, built in 1831 to replace the old chantry bridge. At the time of the photograph tolls were no longer collected, but as yet there is no motor traffic. Orde House is to the right, and this belonged to Mr. Orde of Nunnykirk.

Mr. Orde was the proud owner of Beeswing, a race horse of national renown and popularity. She gave her name to the hostelry at Morpeth where she stayed on her way to retirement in 1842 at Nunnykirk, the Orde's country house, which was improved at this time by John Dobson.

Beeswing, in the course of her career, won 51 out of 64 races (1835-42), and 24 gold cups. She was 10 years old when she went to stud and produced, among other foals, Newminster and Nunnykirk, both to become classic winners. She was mobbed by well-wishers during her stay at Beeswing Yard.

45.   The market place is shown empty, apart from one girl. The town hall has a new (1870) front, protected by iron railings. In 1903 a new market was opened with access from Grey's Yard by the clock tower. Forty pens each held 30 beasts and there was an open yard for 200.

46.   The Hollon Fountain was erected in 1885 by public subscription in honour of R. W. Hollon of York, who married Mary Trotter of Morpeth. She died in 1877 after 25 years of marriage, and in her memory he left money to provide for 13 goodly women and 12 men – a tea on 5 November and supplies of beef and coal.

47. This shows the characteristic style of Vanbrugh with the deep cuttings in the masonry and the very attractive ironwork protecting the windows. The town hall, damaged by fire, was rebuilt at the expense of the Earl of Carlisle. He also provided books for the Mechanics' Institute Library.

48.   The market square, again empty, reveals the cobbled standing. There is a trough for cattle and a waterspout in front of the Hollon Fountain. The basins above are for human use. At this time temperance was important, through the influenc of Lady Carlisle. However, there are three hostelries to the left of the town hall – *Turk's Head, George and Dragon* and *Earl Grey*.

49.   By contrast, a busy market scene. The Hollon Fountain (1885) is a useful aid to dating and Watson's Corner is stil standing. It was demolished in 1905 to make way for the Y.M.C.A. building. A canopy for the fishmarket is attached to the clock tower.

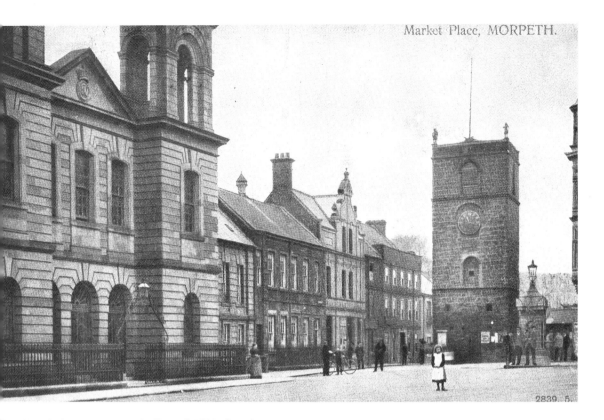

2839. 5.

0.   The clock tower was not built until 1604, though
was constructed of medieval stone and heightened in
705 to house a peal of six bells, presented by Major
eneral Main, M.P. for Morpeth and Governor of
erwick. Built in Cromwell's time, Berwick church
as no tower and Berwick did not elect General Main.
ence Berwick bells are heard in Morpeth.

1.   The clock originally had one hand, so there are
ur spaces between the numbers to tell the quarter
urs. The clock came from Bothal Castle, which once
oused the bark for Morpeth tanners. Bells were rung
r various municipal purposes and the curfew was
ing at 8 p.m. for centuries. For a time the tower was
sed as a lock-up for offenders.

52. The clock tower restricts the entrance to Oldgate, which was more of a residential area than Bridge Street. To the right is Bede Place, the Catholic meeting place before St Robert's church was built opposite. The children seem to have moved while the photograph was taken, *c*.1900.

Oldgate St. Morpeth.

53. Oldgate looking to the river, the narrow bridge and Auburn Place. The post office is on the right. There is a man with a bicycle and two swans sit in the street. The arched entrance was into Pear Tree Yard.

Another view of Oldgate, showing that some houses had an extra storey added. A high cart is waiting outside a shop. The narrow bridge can be seen in the distance with the ford to the left by Matheson's Gardens. Collingwood House is beyond the trees to the right.

55. Collingwood House: 'Here lived the family of Vice Admiral Lord Collingwood, and he spent the few and short periods of repose snatched from long and arduous service afloat. 'Whenever I think how I am to be happy again my thoughts carry me back to Morpeth' (Collingwood). The tablet above the door of the house with these words was erected by the Corporation of Morpeth in 1905, 100 years after Trafalgar.

56. A large monument was erected at Tynemouth in honour of Collingwood, and the guns of his ship the *Royal Sovereign* are on display below his statue.

57. An old picture of Matheson's House which overlooks the Wansbeck. The Mathesons were gardeners and nurserymen for some 300 years. The rebuilt house carries little figures at either end of the shop window with the dates 1689 and 1889. The extensive gardens were very much admired, and the greatest treasure in the house was Collingwood's waistcoat.

58. Collingwood planted acorns on the other side of the river – oak was the material for ships. Here can be seen St Robert's church, built on his land, Collingwood House and Matheson's rebuilt house. The iron girder and lattice bridge was built in 1872, after a suspension bridge collapsed for the second time in 1870.

Chain Bridge, Morpeth

59. This postcard is captioned 'the chain bridge', but seems to depict the bridge that replaced it in 1872. It shows the width of the river. In 1826 there was only the chantry bridge, but also several sets of stepping stones. Baptism for a true Morpethian was to have fallen into the river, and deaths from drowning were not unusual.

60. Morpeth's suspension bridge. The extent of Matheson's gardens is shown and also the woods along the Wansbeck. There is a pathway along the east bank of the river, but the west bank was steep and dangerous. The stony spreads from the river were called 'stanners' and changes continually occurred because of floods.

61. This view from Castle Woods over the town shows the extent of gardens and orchards, with high retaining walls for protection. It would be especially beautiful in blossom time. The spire of St Robert's, the tower of St James's, and the chimney of the County Lunatic Asylum can be seen.

62. We return to the busy market place on market day. The traps or light personal vehicles are ranged in front of the town hall. The butter and corn market is inside. Groups are gossiping, but the auctioneer stands on his platform by the Hollon Fountain surrounded by cattlemen.

63. This view is from market square, looking along a very dirty Bridge Street where an early model of car is parked. The *Earl Grey* is the first hostelry and the next, *George and Dragon*, appeals to cyclists. The *Queen's Head Hotel* beyond the car has not yet been 'modernised'.

64. Further along Bridge Street with St George's church, built in 1861, overlooking the bridge. The bay windows of th *Black Bull* provide views of the street both ways. Gas lighting is evident, and some of the shop fronts are impressive, wit carved brackets and canopies.

65. This card is postmarked 1907, and shows the Y.M.C.A. building being erected on the site of Watson's Corner: the scaffolding is still in place. The new building overpowers the clock tower and challenges the town hall for prominence. A number of delivery vehicles are parked in the street.

66. A fine picture showing the market place from the corner of Newgate Street. The building on the corner has blind windows of the window tax period. It also has a parapet and was probably built shortly after the 1689 fire which destroyed many houses.

67.   In Bridge Street on the right next to the Old Gaol is Wight's Coach Works, established in 1798. An advertisement stresses well-seasoned timber and first-class workmen for making 'Waggonettes, Dog-carts, Gigs, Sparkenhoes, Tilburys, Rustics and other cars built to order'. New and second-hand carriages of all kinds were always on sale. The firm's mott is 'Phoenix arises after the fire'.

68.   Another view of Bridge Street with groups of cattle in front of residences. A boy regards the scene from the seat of a light farm vehicle not in Wight's list. The *Black Bull* and St George's church are towards the centre of the picture.

This view of the same area shows horse vehicles but no cattle. Gas lamps are evident, but the gas works is beyond the trees. e shop on the right with the prominent brackets is that of George B. Grey.

A close-up photograph of the shop showing advertisements for George Grey's wares. To modern display artists the p windows are overcrowded. 'There is a Great Sale now proceeding and Bargains are to be had in Furniture, Household peries, Men's and Boys' Clothing, Ladies' and Children's Coats, Costumes, Blouses and Skirts, also all kinds of Boots l Shoes.'

71. A view from Oliver's Mill showing the Chantry on the left and St George's church. The Telford Bridge, built in 1831, comes between them. Thomas Telford was the engineer, John Dobson the architect and Thomas King the builder. The toll gate was at the south end. The old weir stood at an angle to the river from St George's to a point on the bottom right of the picture. The central pier of the medieval bridge supports an iron bridge of 1864.

72. St. George's Presbyterian church occupied the site of the manorial mill. It replaced the chapel that had been used for 150 years in Cottingwood Lane. This was Horsley's chapel. John Horsley, who died in 1732, was the author of one of the finest works ever written on Roman Britain.

73. John Horsley has no known grave in Morpeth and this plaque on St George's church is his only monument. It was erected in 1932, 200 years after his death and the publication of his great work, 'to preserve his memory in the town where he lived and taught'.

74. The county gaol and court-house. The county gaol was built on the south side of the river between 1822 and 1829 to the designs of John Dobson, who based his plans on Edward I's Welsh castles. The gatehouse has battlements and the prison was surrounded by walls more than 20 ft. high.

75. A full ground plan of the gaol showing the containing wall and the apartments for various types of prisoners, including debtors. Commitments were made after proceedings in the court-house. One hundred years ago the gaol ceased to be used, but the courthouse operated until 1980. The police still have quarters behind the courthouse.

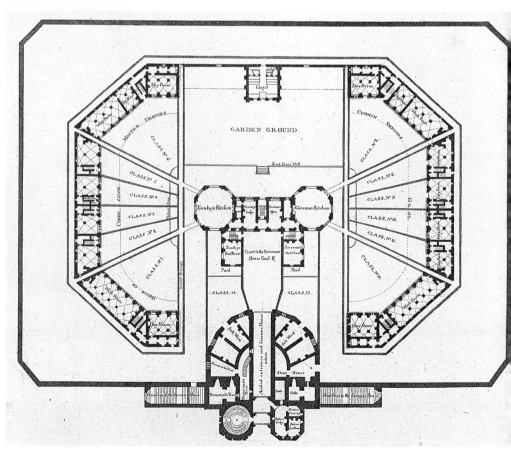

76. An attractive scene about 1900 showing that the prison walls had gone. Telegraph wires have appeared and the cottage in the castle grounds appears on the hill. The snowy road has seen much traffic – towards Newcastle or to the railway station. The railway connection from London to Edinburgh was completed in 1849.

In 1875 the last two
soners were executed in
rpeth. When the prison
s disused, the outer walls
re demolished for
ilding stone. In 1911
osehill Council School
s built on part of the site.
was intended to take 200
ls and 245 boys. During
rld War One the
mises were occupied by
ops.

78. Looking past the court-house to Castle Square, where the trees planted in 1887 for the Queen's Jubilee are quite small. Horse-drawn vehicles were used to transport people and goods between the railway station and the town. Contours as well as councillors kept the railway from entering closely into the populated area.

79. Children enjoying the snow on the road near the *Sun Inn*. St Mary's lychgate can be seen and the Rectory is hidden behind the trees on the left. It is interesting to note that both the parish church and railway station are 'out of town'.

. This interesting sketch made about 1800 shows on the left the Rectory which had been rebuilt in Georgian style. It
cks the later extensions of the Rev. Francis Grey. St Mary's has no lychgate and the higher ground behind the church
wer has no trees. The Bolland monument, 33 ft. high, would have been a landmark had it been erected by this time.

1. The old gaol in Bridge Street was built in 1704 and embodied an earlier tower of Lord Dacre. The Earl of Carlisle
eased it to the Sheriff of Northumberland. In 1822 two prisoners, found guilty of highway robbery, were publicly hanged
n the Gaol Quay near the Wansbeck. From 1829 it was used for coach building and later as a brewery.

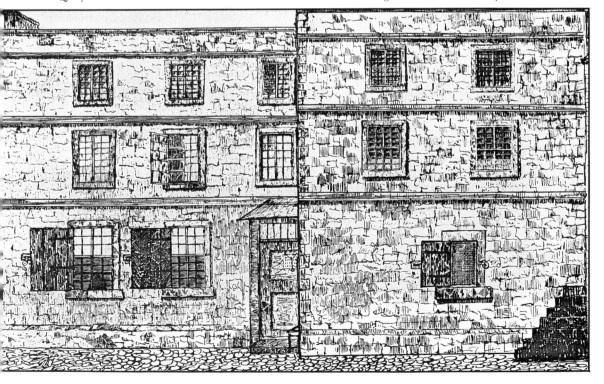

82.   The plan of Morpeth in 1826, which shows how the housing was concentrated on the three main streets. The medieval plan of the burgages can be seen. There are two bridges – the chain bridge and chantry bridge – and three sets of stepping stones. Three mills are shown and the new prison, recently erected.

83. The house shown here is No. 4 Castle Square, and the *Joiners Arms* is to the left. The horse-drawn van, Peek Frean, is probably delivering biscuits there. The date of the photograph is *c.*1890. This can be gauged from the size of the trees planted for the 1887 Jubilee. The occupier of the house was Thomas Waters, auctioneer and agent.

84. A vehicle from the *Queen's Head Hotel* plied regularly between the town and the station to carry passengers, luggage and merchandise. This two-horse vehicle is shown waiting at the station with driver, passenger and porters posing for the photograph.

85. The Doric portico of Mitford Hall, designed by John Dobson. The squire, Bertram Mitford, stands with his wife Brenda, daughter of Canon Macleod, who may well have taken the photograph. The car is probably a Daimler, and the four men are Tom Renton, Bob Brown, Tom Hall and David Dunbar. The butler was Mr. Rapkin.

86. The last passenger train to Rothbury. In 1872 this had been intended as yet another route out to the Border, but Rothbury became the terminus, serving Sir William Armstrong and his visitors. The photograph was taken in 1952, but the locomotive is a veteran. Morpeth station was a junction for lines from Rothbury, Scots Gap, Blyth and the coast.

7. Morpeth was also a railway centre for goods traffic. Many cattle came by train and there was extensive carriage of al from mines to the staiths at Blyth and on the Tyne. This engine is pulling a string of coal waggons. The old footbridge as been replaced.

88. Morpeth station is a substantial Victorian building, characteristic of the impressive railway architecture of the era. A bridge to the left crosses the main road, and the road to the right leads to Park House Farm. The old station buildings opposite testify to a time when there were two stations – another for the Blyth and Tyne Railway.

89. The platforms were sheltered by canopies supported by fine iron columns with decorative work. The large building opposite is the goods shed. Morpeth has seen many famous locomotives pass, including *Mallard*, the record holder of speed for steam locomotives. This was the route of the L.N.E.R. *Flying Scotsman* and *Talisman*.

On Morpeth station, built into the wall on the ...form side, is a map of the N.E. Railway as it was in ...5. It consists of glazed tiles set in a frame and it has ...n preserved for its historical interest. This main ... line is undergoing a further change at present – ...trification.

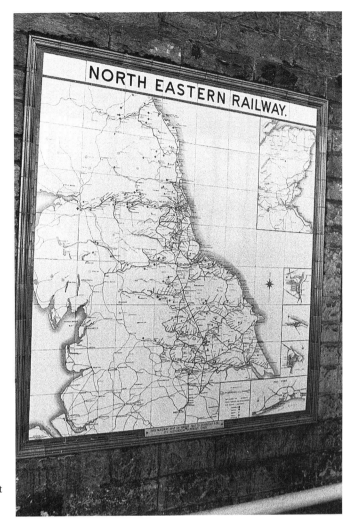

Along the line near the viaduct at Park House ...m is a 'gin-gan'. At one time these buildings were ...mon, and were used to provide cover for horses at ...er end of a pivoted beam, turning a wheel to ...vide power for the machinery in the barn.

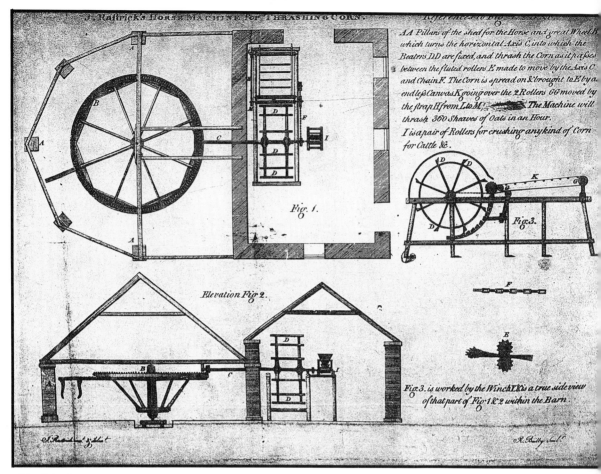

References to Fig. 1 &c.

AA Pillars of the shed for the Horse and great Wheel B, which turns the horizontal Axis C, into which the Beaters DD are fixed, and thrash the Corn as it passes between the fluted rollers E made to move by the Axis C and Chain F. The Corn is spread on & brought to E by a endless Canvas K roving over the 2 Rollers GG moved by the strap H from L to M. The Machine will thrash 360 Sheaves of Oats in an Hour.
I is a pair of Rollers for crushing any kind of Corn for Cattle &c.

Fig. 1.

Fig. 3.

Elevation Fig. 2.

Fig. 3. is worked by the Winch. It is a true side view of that part of Fig. 1 & 2 within the Barn.

92.   John Rastrick, born 1738, lived in Morpeth and invented a threshing machine. He trained his son John who also became an engineer. John Junior was engaged on railway projects, and knew the Stephensons well. As a judge at the Rainhill Trials (1829) he favoured *The Rocket*. In 1830 this locomotive killed William Huskisson, once M.P. for Morpeth.

3. Crossing the Wansbeck near Park House is the Morpeth or Bothal Viaduct. It was completed by Robert Stephenson in 1849. The permanent way is 100 ft. above the waters of the Wansbeck – a fine piece of engineering.

94.   Another view of the viaduct gives a better impression of the style and strength of the construction. The 'great ston quarry' of the 1738 map is to the right, and there was also coal mining in the area. There were two water mills in the vicinity. The Wansbeck winds between high, tree-covered banks and is a place of great natural beauty.

95.   The Lady Chapel is further along the valley and probably housed a hermit in medieval times. It measured 25 ft. by 16 ft. and fell into decay. William Turner knew it and saw the orobanche 'so rare an herbe ... that I never saw it in all Englande, but in Northumberland where it is called Newchapel flower'.

96. The Lady Chapel was restored in 1887 for Queen Victoria's Jubilee; the Lady's Well was also restored to use as were several springs in the valley. There was some earlier carving of a coat of arms on the rock under an arch. Tomlinson (1888) speaks of 'Ye Jubilee Well' 1887, and describes it as 'one of the loveliest spots of Northumberland'.

97. By way of contrast there was much mining in the area, and at the top of Whorral Bank are the remains of a disused colliery. The water that has collected in the galleries is pumped out for industrial purposes. There are depressions of bell pits in the neighbouring fields.

98. This bridge at Low Stanners was transferred in 1932 by steam engine haulage from Oldgate. It was here that the waggonway from Netherton crossed the river by wooden staithes, and coal was carried here for the gas works. This would have been the terminus of the canal proposed in 1738.

99. Thompson's shop stood on Wellway at the junction with Staithes Lane. This was where the Cottingburn met the old mill leat underground. Waters could be heard in the shop with its unusual rounded corner. The *Old Red Bull* is to the left and Wellwood House to the right.

00. Morpeth Y.M.C.A. Bowling Club, 1925. Back row: R. Naisby, E. E. McRobb, G. W. Middlemass, G. Turnbull,
. H. Atkinson, Mrs. G. H. Atkinson, F. Rowe, D. C. Major, G. Charlton, G. V. Smith, and M. Henderson; front row.
. E. Waterson, J. T. Watson, W. Bowman, W. Taylor, W. Allen (capt.), T. R. Tully, G. Middlemass, R. Young,
. G. Marshall, and G. M. Stout.

101. In 1846, to provide for the expanding northern part of the town, another church had been built – the church of St James the Great. The moving spirit behind this was Rev. Francis Grey, son of Earl Grey and married to Elizabeth, daughter of the Earl of Carlisle. The church was designed by Benjamin Ferry in Norman style, like a church in Sicily. The building incorporated a school.

102. This building in Manchester Street was the Wesleyan Methodist chapel. It was built in 1884 in Gothic style to seat 400 people. It replaced a chapel of 1820 on the same site and an earlier one founded by the Countess of Huntingdon. John Wesley visited Morpeth a score of times between 1748 and 1786.

103. Another building in Cottingwood Lane which served as a school was Horsley's chapel (1720). Horsley was both a Presbyterian minister and a teacher. The building was used as a school dining hall, dancing hall and Red Cross centre. It has since been converted into a residence, 'Kirkville'.

104. Benjamin Ferry was responsible for another fine building (1858-9) in Cottingwood Lane – the new King Edward VI Grammar School. It survived the century but because listing of Victorian buildings comes last to the North, it was demolished and replaced by a nondescript modern structure.

105. This photograph shows the pupils of Standard IV of St James's Church of England School in 1894. The school was built adjacent to the church through the efforts of Rev. Francis Grey, in the same architectural scheme with the grammar school and church. The school was demolished after the 1968 floods.

106. Grammar School boys sitting in order on the steps in front of the main door with attendant staff. The date is 1888, and it seems to be summer to judge from the vegetation and the boaters. The headmaster was William Davidson, the second master was James Kenner and the third was Frederick Lake.

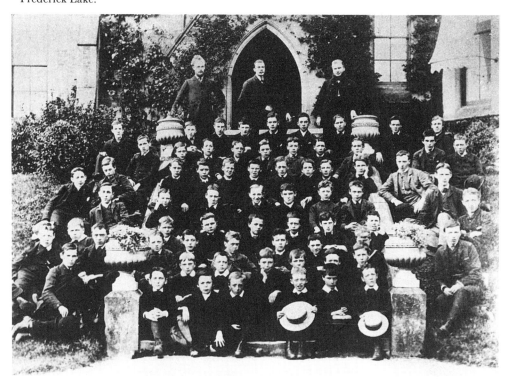

107. Cottingwood Lane, though narrow, was very much used – there were two schools, market gardens and the County Lunatic Asylum on its route. There were also brickworks and deep clay pits had been excavated. The old windmill overlooked the site.

108. The old hemmel was one of the buildings on Cottingwood Common which provided shelter for the cattle or persons caught in a storm. The land was used for grazing, and at one time there was a race course in the area. Horse racing was later transferred to the south-west side of the town, on the Common there.

109. A picture of the County Lunatic Asylum. Tomlinson wrote: 'At Cottingwood, on a lofty site, is the County Lunatic Asylum, a large and commodious building of red brick, in the Italian style, with woods and gardens around it. It was opened in 1859 and has accommodation for over 800 patients.' It is now called St George's Hospital.

110. East Cottingwood, the doctors' part of St George's Hospital, which with Northgate caters for several thousand patients. The modern tendency has been to develop separate housing units, and more recently still to put patients back into the community. A great deal of local employment is provided by the hospital and the employees have various teams for sports.

. Cottingwood Lane leads to Wansbeck
use. Rebuilt in Gothic style with battlements,
as the residence of Joseph Crawhall Senior,
ist and angler. He published *The Completest
gling Boke* at Morpeth in 1859. His son John,
mous artist, was born here in 1861. Later the
mises were occupied by the Girls' High
ool (1905), from 1948 called Grammar
ool.

2. This shows the castellated front entrance
Newgate Street. The school premises
luded Bon Accord, a fine 18th-century house,
me of Mary Trotter. Niece of Dr. William
otter, she married Richard Hollon, chemist
d Lord Mayor of York. The houses had
ractive gardens. In 1967 the girls moved to
new school and these premises became the
achers' Centre.

113. Photographs of the girls have been difficult to obtain. This is a form of 35, taken in 1932. Some of the girls have gym slips and others are wearing summer dresses. The school took paying and scholarship pupils. Northumberland now has a three-tier system of First, Middle and High Schools. All senior students are in one High School.

114. The west side of Newgate Street overlooks the Wansbeck and the houses have stepped or terraced gardens, leading down to the river. They had fruit trees, lilac bushes and here is shown a solitary Lombardy poplar. The stepping stones are visible and also St Robert's church. The houses on the right were built on the Stanners *c.*1890.

115. Gardens and houses can be seen from the other side of the river. The large building on the right the Workhouse, erected in 1868 for 150 inmates. It was five storeys high and brick built. During the W it was used by the county council. In 1951 it was demolished and the telephone exchange took its plac

The image shows arcading with the inscription: LORD · I · DAVE · LOVED · THE · DABITATION · OF · THY · HOUSE · AND · THE · PLACE · WHERE · THINE

116.   This elegant arcading on the western approach to St James's church was built in 1890 as a memorial to Rev. Francis Grey, who was for 48 years Rector of Morpeth and instrumental in getting the church built. The columns are of Frosterley marble and the ironwork was made by Swinney Brothers of Morpeth. Originally there were flower beds in front.

117. Stoker's butcher's shop has served the public in Morpeth for one hundred years and more. The style of the shop fro has not altered – the door still opens in two sections. The carcases here are on display for the benefit of the photographer and would not stay long like this. They would have to be chopped and carved into pieces.

118. A number of gentlemen are talking near the *Old Nag's Head* in Newgate Street. Only one wing of it has yet been 'tudorised'. The shop next door was Jacksons, painters and decorators. Dance & Carr were caterers, later moving to the Y.M.C.A. buildings, where one could buy a jar of Cumbrian cream for 6d.

119. The Y.M.C.A. buildings, finished in 1905. The doorhead is carved 'G B B 1905', referring to Alderman Bainbridge who had the L-shaped premises built. The other wing goes into Oldgate with a carriage entrance. The building is four storeys high plus an attic and dominates the square. Fine views are obtained from the upper windows.

NEWGATE ST MORPETH

120.   This is a fine view back up Newgate Street – road works in progress even then! The whole scene, however, is very
leisurely. Two onlookers are leaning on the Hollon Fountain, which also has a bicycle leaning against it. The last two shops
on the left are in the Y.M.C.A. buildings.

. The *Morpeth Herald* office, once the
be and Anchor Inn, keeps one of the old
p fronts intact with a step up above
at were dirty streets. Printers from
1, the Mackay family printed the
ald from 1854 till 1983, when the
eeddale Press took over. Back
nbers of the paper are a repository of
al news and history.

. This 1948 photograph shows what
as like in the *Morpeth Herald* Yard, with
bled street and congested buildings.
ives a glimpse of the areas that were
wded with people and rarely
otographed. A lot of these buildings
e now been demolished.

123. This photograph shows the brothers Dixon of Molesden, near Morpeth, *c*.1925. They were carpenters and cartwrights, serving the surrounding farms, getting timbers from Wrights of Morpeth and ironwork from Swinneys. They repaired farm equipment and also made coffins. Their work was said to be first class, but they took their time and coul be expensive.

24. Their house was at one time a tower and the back wall was very thick. The outbuildings were the workshop and
table. Cartwheels can be seen and there is a barrel to catch the rainwater. The garden has a combination of hedge, fence
id wall with fruit bushes and beehives within. There were lilacs too.

125.   In Bridge Street before 1905 we see the array of shops and, rather interestingly, the horse-drawn vehicle carrying lamp oil, although the town has gas lighting. Shops include Soulsby's clothiers, Bowman and Garvie paperhangers, and the *Herald* office.

126.   Another popular event to be recorded was the 'Beating of the Bounds' on or near St Mark's Day, 25 April. The civil officials attended with symbols of office – the company consisted almost entirely of men and boys. Here the progress was on foot, but it was often done by horses, finishing with races upon the Common. This photograph was taken *c*.1890.

27. Royal visits were great occasions. Edward VII visited Morpeth in 1905 and this photograph shows the Prince of Wales in 1923, hat in hand listening to the town clerk's speech of welcome. Alderman W. S. Sanderson stands behind him and other dignitaries stand nearby. Flags decorate the crowded street and people are looking out from all the windows of the square.

128.   In 1933 outside the garage is what became a best-selling model Ford car. This is a sales promotion run a
it is interesting to notice gentlemen in different attire. One is wearing plus-fours, the garb of golfers, and
Mr. Jennings wears a bowler hat. The old petrol pumps are in the background.

FUNERAL AT MORPE
MISS E.W. DAVI

GREATER LOVE HATH NO MAN
THAN THIS, THAT A MAN LAY
DOWN HIS LIFE FOR HIS FRIENDS
St JOHN XV CHP XIII VERSE.

EMILY WILDING
DAVISON
BORN OCT 11TH 1872
DIED JUNE 8TH 1913.
DEEDS NOT WORDS.

ALFRED NORRIS
DAVISON
SON OF
C. E. DAVISON
WHO DIED AT VANCOUVER B.C.
JANUARY 26TH 1918
AGED 45 YEARS.

THE LORD THY GOD IS WITH THEE
WITHERSOEVER THOU GOEST
JOSHUA I CHP 9 V

ERECTED
N AFFECTIONATE MEMORY OF
SARAH SETON
THE BELOVED WIFE OF
CHARLES E DAVISON
OF WINTON HOUSE MORPETH
WHO DIED 30TH APRIL 1866
AGED 44 YEARS

CHARLES E DAVISON
WHO DIED 7TH FEBRUARY 1893
AGED 70 YEARS
AT REST.

ALSO MARGARET
WIFE OF THE ABOVE
WHO DIED AT LONGHORSLEY
2ND FEBRUARY 1911
AGED 69 YEARS

THY WILL BE DONE.

129. In the summer of 1913 Emily Davison
the suffragette, died from injuries received
on Derby Day, when she went under the
King's horse, 'Amner'. She was brought b
train to Morpeth for burial, and this
photograph shows her funeral procession t
St Mary's church. Thousands of people
attended and she is regarded as a
Morpethian.

130. 'It was one of the biggest days that
Morpeth has ever seen.' The late Harry
Jackson, a boy at the *Sun Inn*, said they sold
5,000 drinks – beer at 1d., spirits at 3d. Mar
people came on bicycles. An appropriate
monument was erected to Emily in St Mary
churchyard, and it has recently been
refurbished. The Bolland monument stand
higher.

31.   Thomas Burt was secretary of the Northumberland Miners for 48 years and M.P. for Morpeth for 40 years. Miners' picnics were often held at Blyth, occasionally at Morpeth – in 1900, 1903, 1906 and 1913. Here Burt is seen speaking to the crowd. M.P.s such as Ramsay Macdonald, Keir Hardie, Charles Fenwick and Philip Snowden attended.

132.   At Winton House are the Havelock Cup winners – Morpeth Team B Company 1897 of the Northumberlan[
First Volunteer Battalion Fusiliers. Some of these would later be involved in the South African or Boer War.

133. 'The soldier.' This snapshot, called a Souvenir from France, was captioned 'This was the laugh that cost me the price of a new plate'.

134. The war memorial carries the names of those who fell in two world wars. About 11 November every year, after a remembrance service in one of the Morpeth churches, a procession is made to this monument for another service. Mafeking Park has been so reduced by road changes that it is now no more than a roundabout.

135.   A double row of terraced houses called Pretoria Avenue is a reminder of the Boer War. A stone in the wall of a house near the river gives the date 1900 and states that it was laid by Ethel Lee. The avenue has a slight curve. The houses have front gardens and enclosed backs and are in an attractive situation.

36.   Panoramic photograph looking east. There is grazing land on the south slope and gardens on the other side down o the river with protective walls. Beyond the town hall rows of buildings run down to the river. On the horizon, fringed y woods, can be seen St George's Hospital.

Price's Banks, Morpeth.

137. Up a zig-zag path from Oldgate bridge, called Kerly Kews, were the so-called Victorian Pleasure Gardens, and shown here is Price's cottage part way up the bank. Here teas were provided for school parties and others. Higher still a the top of the bank was a flat field used for sports and entertainments.

138. A splendid view of the south bank of the river where there is as yet no promenade. The fields, trees and hedges are shown. In the distance can be seen the castle and on the far le Ha' Hill, the original castle mound, later to b part of Carlisle Park (1916).

. The activity of the river has
ded the southern bank and
osited it on the other side. This
cess was stopped by the
lding of a river wall and
menade in the 1930s as part of
rlisle Park. The top of the court-
se is visible.

. A delightful picture of little
s following a footpath and
king flowers. The path descends
he Postern Burn and makes for
castle. The castle is inhabited,
the curtain walls of the
losure are covered with ivy.

141.   Another rural scene in the fields towards Mitford, as depicted by Canon Macleod. Farm workers – a man, two women and a boy – are sitting under the hedge enjoying their 'bait'. It is unusual to see smiling faces, difficult in photographs of that time because of the length of exposure needed.

142.   Another of Canon Macleod's photographs shows a female group posing at a wicket gate near Mitford Bridge. Mitford is two miles distant from Morpeth, and the wooded Wansbeck valley always provides a pleasant walk. The *Plough Inn* is seen beyond the bridge and further up the hill was the smithy.

143. Canon Macleod was a member of the Y.M.C.A. Morpeth camera club, and this bridge was a favourite spot for photographs. Sheep were dipped here before they went for shearing. It was a favoured place for children paddling and he recorded Sunday School parties enjoying themselves in the water.

144. Back at Morpeth the stepping stones were a perennial attraction, and many a boy must have returned home with wet feet. St Robert's church stands on what was Collingwood's garden. He called the walk along the river bank his 'quarter deck'. At the bottom of the garden is a gazebo or summer house.

145.   Another attractive view of the river shows the cattle grazing on the south side and walkers taking the river path. The extensive orchard and gardens can be seen with their protective walls. The river has piled up silt and gravel on the northern side. Neither bank is protected by a wall.

146.   This very fine picture shows a gipsy encampment on the waste land on the north bank of the river below Matheson's gardens. Along the river is the lattice iron bridge and beyond it looms the Workhouse. St Robert's spire is prominent and the river seems very still.

147. This photograph must have been taken after 1932 since another girder bridge has been erected at Oldgate, though the ford still has to be used for heavy traffic. The previous bridge was moved to Gas House Lane. This bridge was replaced in 1974.

148. By the time this photograph was taken Carlisle Park has been created and the Promenade has been built on the south bank (1936). The Elliott Bridge was built in 1925 by public subscription and was rebuilt in 1982. It was opened by Sir William Elliott, M.P. Boating became a popular form of entertainment on this part of the Wansbeck.

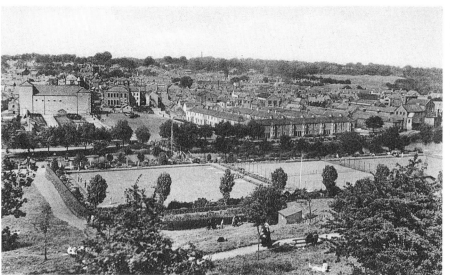

149. Attractive gardens laid out in Carlisle Park with paths and seats for visitors. The bowling green and tennis courts attracted sportspeople. A cinema, the Coliseum, has appeared in the town and Baysland flats have been built. Oliver's Mill stands high on the right of the picture.

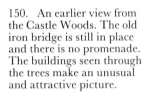

150. An earlier view from the Castle Woods. The old iron bridge is still in place and there is no promenade. The buildings seen through the trees make an unusual and attractive picture.

151. This photograph taken from the court-house in about 1922 shows the close packed housing around. Oliver's Mill is seen mid-right. The long line of buildings in the Baysland area was a post-war addition to housing. Pantiles are prominent on the roofs of the houses. The river can be seen to the left.

52. Morpeth Diamond Jubilee Band, 1897. The bandsmen are not in uniform, but variously dressed, and no doubt performed with great gusto when they joined the assembly in the Market Place on Jubilee Day and took part in the procession.

153. Jubilee Day was a great occasion – the Civic dignitaries, the Northumberland Fusiliers a⟨
others met in the bedecked square. Bells were rung and cannon fired, followed by an official speec⟨
and the singing of the national anthem with orchestra and handbells. There was feasting for all – i⟨
the public houses, workhouse and marquees. There were sports and entertainments for childre⟨
and adults, as well as a procession and band.

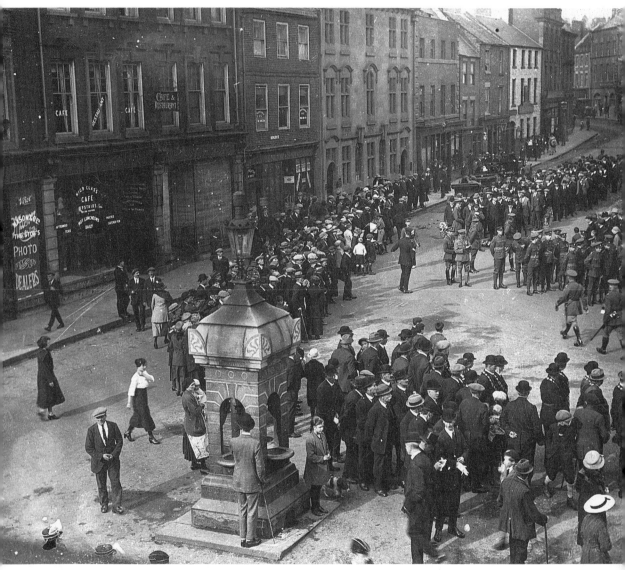

154.   A Remembrance Day ceremony very soon after the War finished. Various groups are assembling with wreaths, both civic leaders and the military. People are 'forming fours' for the procession to the war memorial.

155. Fair Day in the Market Square with stalls and amusements. Fairs were held in Morpeth on Wednesday, Thursday and Friday a week before Whitsun, and on Tuesday, Wednesday, Thursday and Friday during the first week of September when the local races took place.

156. The Market Square in the 1920s, with the Playhouse Cinema behind the Hollon Fountain. Note the tricyclist in the foreground. The old buildings on the right housed the Trustee Savings Bank.

157. The Market Place again, with the front of the town hall and a long stretch of Bridge Street with shop awnings. A solid-tyred bus appears on one side and a delivery van on the other.

158. Soulsby's shop in Bridge Street next to the Borough of Morpeth Corporation Offices. Soulsby's had a reputation for good quality hard-wearing men's clothing, catering for the ordinary man rather than the fashionable. The aim of the window display was to show as much as possible rather than to be artistic.

49. A delightful photograph of Hermann Pluss Hill's catering place, showing the wheel of a bicycle as a symbol. It was the meeting place of the C.T.C. and all cyclists were specially welcome. A large three-tier cake is visible and hot-cross buns suggest Eastertide.

50. James Whittle, Chemist and Druggist of 20 Bridge Street, may well have provided the materials for the taking of this photoraph himself. He advertised 'Amateur Photographers Plates and Films Developed, Printed and Enlarged – Dark Room'. This photograph, which he might have taken, was part of his advertisement in the Official Town Guide of 1908. Soulsby's and Hill's appeared in the same Guide.

161. This was thought to be Mafeking Night, but it was taken on 4 July 1903 at the village of Whalton, near Morpeth.
An annual event there was the Baalfire or Midsummer Fire, a pagan relic of the old Midsummer Eve. When the bonfire
was lit people danced around it to the sound of a fiddler's music and the daring leapt through it.

162. The old Treasury of the seven groups of gilds of Old Morpeth, in the town hall. All seven aldermen had to be present at the same time with seven keys, so that the seven locks could be opened and the lid lifted. Now closed and a symbol of the past, it is called the Hutch.

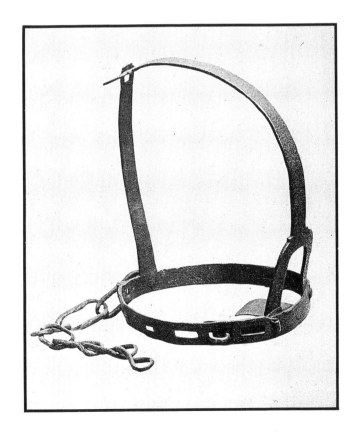

163. 'The Branks' are kept in the town hall. This was a bridle used for the punishment of 'scolds', or nagging women. 'December 3 1741 Elizabeth, wife of George Holborn, punished with the branks for two hours at the Market Cross, for scandalous & opprobrious language to several persons in town, as well as to the bailiffs'. These 'bailiffs' were the magistrates who tried her!

164. An attractive picture of the trees on the banks of the Postern Burn, a deep ravine that divides the Norman castle from the later castle with gatehouse. Oaks are a reminder of Morpeth's tanning industry. This land became part of Carlisle Park with delightful walks and gardens. The park is much appreciated by residents and visitors and has won awards for flowers.

165. Morpeth was once famous as a market for black cattle, driven from the hills and from Scotland. They are not common nowadays, and after hundreds of years there is no market in the town. Cattle come direct to the abattoir.

6. (*right*) Wheatsheaf Yard. This interesting building ...d a Dutch-type gable and was roofed with pantiles. It ...obably dated to the reign of William III and was rebuilt ...er the fire of 1689. The buildings were of attractive ...ck and the bottom windows had iron bars. The front ...ilding has been demolished. It had a vaulted cellar and ...vell in the yard.

7a. & b. (*below*) Window brackets were once general ...naments to shop fronts, two supporting the canopy. Only a ...w have survived modernisation. Similar figures were ...rved inside churches or on gargoyles outside. These two ...amples provide an interesting contrast – one is smiling, ...arded and benevolent, the other is thin, cramped and ...iserable. Perhaps they depict the fall of man – the plenty of ...e Garden of Eden and the misery after the fall.

168. The Parochial Hall was built after the 1914-1918 War as a war memorial. Financed by various activities and donations, it was used for all kinds of community purposes. During World War Two it was used by the Y.M.C.A. as an army canteen, and purchased by that organisation in 1965 after they had given up their Oldgate premises.

169. West High House Farm must be one of the oldest buildings in Morpeth. The house was converted into two cottages and then used for animals. It is built partly of stone but mostly of hand-made bricks, and roofed with pantiles. Some of the old windows are still in place.

170. No. 105 Newgate Street is probably 17th-century or earlier, with thick walls and stone from
Newminster. The windows have been altered and a third storey added. This most attractive portico
was added in the 18th-century, with pillars, an ogee hood and neat fanlight. The scraper is a
reminder of dirty streets, horses and cattle.

171. This view underneath the arches of Telford's Bridge indicates the passing of time and the waters of the Wansbeck. Stones are brought down and the traffic passes above. Oliver's Mill works no longer and the medieval bridge is a footbridge only, but the old pier remains, having divided the waters for more than 700 years.

172. The footbridge was restored in 1869 by Swinney's, whose Ironworks were famous in Morpeth for more than a century. This plaque is now their monument, since their premises have been converted to a supermarket.